Conversational Shrapnel

Caitlin Baker

BookLeaf Publishing

India | USA | UK

Presentation by *BookLeaf Publishing*

Web: www.bookleafpub.com

E-mail: info@bookleafpub.com

ISBN: 9789357612296

First edition 2022

DEDICATION

Dedicated to all my loved ones, who are my muses for better or worse.

ACKNOWLEDGEMENT

Thank you to Kasey and Sarah, who have proof read more of my writing than anyone else.

Seasons

After a long hard winter
You were a fresh spring breeze
Flowing through my window
And bringing me back to life
But
even spring needs to pass
so I guess
It's time for summer now

Fault

Do you ever wonder what you're doing wrong?
Because I do
It makes me want to call all my past lovers
And ask where everything fell apart
I wish I could cover myself in correctional tape
So maybe then I could keep you safe from my
flaws, my mistakes, and my regrets
Because they have a way of ruining things

Let Go

Suddenly,
I realized you weren't coming back.
I should have seen it a long time ago
But i guess i was blinded by love
A love only I was clinging to

And now I'm hurting from a goodbye
That never even happened

No matter how bad it hurts,
I still cling to the stupid idea
and false hope
That you might come back to me

Porcelain

Every time you press your cup to your lips
I find myself wishing I was born made of
porcelain

Rain Storm

It just keeps on raining,
It's like the sky is crying with you, love.
It's like your pain is such a burden
That the universe tried to carry it for you
And even it broke under the weight.

Bagel

She butters my bagel
(And that's not a euphemism,)
With such care
You'd swear it was a religious rite
Except she swore off religion
When they swore to her
That it all happens for a reason.
That makes bile burn at my throat
For even at my most devote
I would never tell a little babe,
Like some kind of Spiritualist sicko,
That it was the will of God
That ripped and bruised
Her unripened fruit
So, maybe that's why,
her house of worship
Is inside me
After all it's the only time
The lord's name will crest her lips
I like to think that means
she has more faith in me
Than in an old dusty book
People use to hide their bigotry.
she takes such care in the mundane
For if there is no afterlife

She cherishes the present a little extra
And is so attentive when doing the small things
Like buttering my bagel

Please, Fix Me

A shrug is not a diagnosis,
'Nothing' is not an treatment,
and ignorance is not medicine
'you should be relieved there is nothing wrong'
No.
Something is wrong
You just don't know what
so you can't treat it
and I just have to deal with it
Pain with no name
no reason
and no end.

Capitalistic Value

when the big shots on tv
talk about what we've lost
during the pandemic
they talk in dollar signs
in job loss
in property values
but how do you measure
missing the first year
of your niece's life
or the last year of your Grandfather's?
How much dollar value can you ascribe
to all the students who lost a year of class?
to the lovers, the families, the friends
who lost uncountable moments with each other?
We will never know
the full extent of what we all truly lost

RED

The color of the warm fluid
that gushes through my veins
and the color of the organ
that continuously works,
pumping to keep me alive.
It's also the color of your favorite shirt
the one that has faded from being washed three
hundred times
and my favorite:
red is the color of your lips
whose colors, thankfully, never fade
no matter how many times I kiss them.

Start Again

They say the best part of breaking up
is starting over again
but beginnings are hard…
The way my room smells like you
(even hours after you've left)
is enough to drive me mad
and it makes me crazy
that are kisses are planned,
not natural and necessary.
It makes me sad that
I don't know all your little quirks yet
and that I can't read your face
with just one glance.
It makes me almost insane
knowing that your body is unexplored terrain
and that your hands
are frightened to touch me.
Beginnings are hard…
but I want to memorize that scent
and kiss you a million times,
until it is necessary.
I want to hear all your stories
until I can read your reactions as well as I know
mine
and I need to know every inch of you
even if it takes all eternity.

Clovers

I look for four leaf clovers in every patch I see
and I've never met a sunset I didn't love
as its colours consumed the sky.
I've got a binder full of stories I have never
completed
and have always longed for wild flowers to grow
from my veins
so I too could be beautiful like a forest.
Before I met you I only cared about pretty words
but now all I can only think about your pretty
face
and how I've never wanted anything as much as
I want you to love me.
That's why I'm telling you these little things
because you make me want to bleed my story on
a page
so you can know every naked part of me

Not Me

Every now and then
I remember how much I love you.
and then my heart grows heavy
and tears paint my cheeks
because I know not once have you thought of
me.
You never think about holding my hand
in a roomful of crowed people or on a busy
street
or brushing my hair behind my ear so you can
see how I'm blushing.
I bet you never think about
the little things that make me smile
or my favorite colours
or the tiny quirks that make me who I am.
I know you never wonder
what it would feel like to press your lips against
mine
or to wake up in my arms, sharing body heat and
tangled sheets,
or know what it feels like to hear me whisper 'I
love you' in your ear.
And that's what breaks my heart...
Because these thoughts cross my mind all the
time.

I think of all the possibilities…
and dream of the impossible.
but the truth is I can't think of love without
thinking of you
and you can't think of love with me.

Sadie

Small hands
tiny toes
pouty lips
nana's nose
Sleepy eyes
room full of love
you're truly sent
from up above
Looking at you
we're all impressed
my heart now lives
outside my chest
Once big sister
now an aunt
I'll nurture the seeds
that you plant
Thank you baby
we needed you
a wish I didn't know I had
come true

Hunger Strike

I imagine its cold out there on the protest line
tonight
as I sit on the sidewalk and wait for my bus.
I imagine you're hungry by now
having started your hunger strike over a day ago
and I feel guilty about the groceries in my hand.
You carry so much,
burdens society has placed on you,
burdens you have no choice but to shoulder.
so you fight.
You are stronger than any person I have ever
known.
You shouldn't have to be,
but you are
and you're out there risking it all
for what is right.
I've never met someone as strong as you are You
are amazing.

Non-consensual Dissemination of Intimate Images

We got over our reservations -
about our bodies, our morals, what our mothers
would say
and hit send.
You smirk and whisper 'nice' to yourself,
saving it for later.
Then things don't go your way
regardless of whose fault it is,
those photos are now your ammo,
your phone a loaded gun.
We cry ourselves to sleep at night
(or don't sleep at all)
knowing there is nothing we can do
because we've seen it happen before
to a friend of a friend.
You gather on message boards,
hiding behind fake names and a keyboard
trading pictures of us
like school boys trade hockey cards
while we are slowly dying

from insults and underserved shame
and a blade that you put in her our hands
because we see no way out.
Our lives are over it seems,
forever altered
while you remain free,
 unscathed,
unaccountable,
unreprimanded
free to do it all over again

Between Like and Love

There is a lexical gap in the English language
as there are no combination of our 26 letters
that allow us to describe the feeling nestled
between
like and love.
There is no word to describe the comfort of
settling into a relationship
that still gives you butterflies
or the attraction you feel on the eleventh date
Like is simply not enough.
Your heart pounds too hard for just
L I K E
But God…
Love seems too big
too heavy
for so early
Fond is truly an understatement
Need sounds ridiculous in your late 20s
Lust can certainly describe the ache I feel
when we're alone in your room
but…

It's more than that too.
There are simply no words to describe
how much I still enjoy about you
or the way it feels to hold your hand in the
crowd
or how I can't wait
to fall in love with you.
So I guess for now,
we'll have to deal with the gap
and say "I ______ you"

Lingerie

It only took two years
for me to forget what it felt like
to be loved by a lover
But here you are:
cooking us breakfast at ten pm
while we're both in lingerie
Your hips are swaying gently
as you sing to yourself
and god…
it's clear that I've been ensnared in your web.
Part of me wants to panic,
to trash and free myself
because I remember how long it takes
to heal a broken heart
and how bitter I can be
But then you're looking at me
those baby blues…
They could probably kill me
and I would let them
because even though I remember how much it
hurt
you remind me how miraculous love feels
how light and magical it can make my life
and how lucky I am
to hear you call me baby

as you kiss my forehead
and make me breakfast at ten pm
while we're both dressed in lingerie

Loop

Sometimes the words spill from my lips
like blood from a gash
and I just can't stop the words
or the churn of anxiety in my gut
and worry racing through my brain,
all endlessly feeding off each other
in a horrible cyclical loop

Kind Strangers

Never again will I take for granted the kindness
of strangers
A kind drunk girl in a bar bathroom
A sweet old man holding the door
A stranger on the bus telling you that you
dropped your wallet
A mystery friend leaving you a surprise.
When illness swept the nation
I think it infected our good will too.

Shake

You made my whole body tremble
With just a single glance
Your eyes lit a fire in the pit of my stomach
Which warmed my body so.
Suddenly being in a room with you was hard
I couldn't stop shaking
And I am not sure I ever will

Salt

McDonalds fries,
The sea,
Mom's cooking,
And tears - proof that salt heals everything